D0809865

grim

FACTS

REALLY GRIM FACTS

Summersdale Publishers Ltd
46 West Street
Chichester
West Sussex
PO19 1RP
UK

www.summersdale.com

Printed and bound by Scotprint, Haddington

ISBN: 978-1-84953-183-2

Substantial discounts on bulk quantities of Summersdale books are available to corporations, professional associations and other organisations. For details telephone Summersdale Publishers on (+44-1243-771107), fax (+44-1243-786300) or email (nicky@summersdale.com).

REALLY

grim

FACTS

TED LEECH

summersdale

CONTENTS

iNTRODUCTiON

Here is a collection of nausea-inducing facts from around the world to completely gross you out, from body facts that will make you itch to food facts that will have you reaching for a bucket. Read on to discover how a pile of poo once saved a woman's life, where maggot ice cream is served on the menu, and which critter produces the smelliest farts – prepare to be amazed and disgusted.

Warning: do not read prior to eating.

REALLY GRIM FOOD FACTS

Many Icelanders refuse to eat their traditional dish, *hákarl*. To prepare it you must acquire the **head** of a shark, **bury** it, leave it for **three months**, dig it up, slice it into strips and **serve**. This pungent delicacy is said to taste of mature cheese.

Always wash your veggies before eating them; even **organic farmers** use some unpalatable substances to fertilise their crops. Animal **urine** is a popular plant booster due to its high nitrogen content, and **ash** and **tobacco** are used to ward off pests.

Caterpillar **fungus** is used in Chinese and Tibetan medicine, and can be served in soup. The fungus grows on insect larvae, **mummifies** the caterpillar and grows as a mushroom from the **caterpillar's forehead**.

The next time you **eat** a doughnut, plate of chips or anything else containing **hydrogenated** fats, consider this: these **fats** are so **thick** they can continue to clog your insides for up to a **year**.

Eggs are a popular food in Asia, particularly **duck** eggs containing **part-developed** ducklings. The shells are removed and the **feathery** contents are **eaten** with onion sauce.

On average, you will consume 12 **pubic hairs** in your **food** per year.

The African Masai people **supplement** their basic diet of cornmeal and cow's milk with a **blood** milkshake. A **sharp** point is used to make a **hole** in the unfortunate cow's vein and the blood is **drained** and **mixed** with milk.

Eating **excessive** amounts of **sugar** can cause **worms** in humans.

A family in Canada dining at a fast-food restaurant were **disgusted** to find that one of their **burgers** contained a whole **rat's head,** still with **eyes** and other **facial** features.

Ukrainians are fond of porcine **delicacies**. One such treat is called *salo*, which is produced by using the **liquids** and fats that drip from an **impaled** pig's head. The soup-like mixture is often eaten **raw**.

There are a number of non-food **contaminants** present in many supermarket foods that by law will **pass inspection** in small quantities. These nasties include rodent **droppings**, hair and **dirt**.

The world's most expensive **coffee**, *kopi luwak* or civet coffee, is made from beans that have passed through the **digestive system** of Sumatran civet cats. The beans are picked out from the cats' **faeces**, cleaned and roasted – yum!

Italy's Casu Frazigu cheese has been deemed **unsafe** to eat. Flies lay eggs on the surface that **hatch** and **burrow** through the cheese, **leaking** out enzymes which make it smell and taste **rotten**. It can only be eaten for a few weeks as the flies become **poisonous** once dead.

A woman eating **clam chowder** in California in 2002 found it more **rubbery** than she expected. She was taken aback when she realised why – there was a **condom** in her chowder!

The food that creates the worst **smells** could well be the cowpea, or 'black-eyed pea'. In addition to a **bad** bout of **farting**, cowpeas have been known to cause indigestion, increased **belching**, diarrhoea, vomiting, bad breath, **constipation** and abdominal discomfort.

The record for eating live **cockroaches** is 36 Madagascar hissing roaches in **60 seconds**, held by a man from Derbyshire, **UK.**

One US woman has kept
a **hamburger** she
purchased from a global
fast-food chain for 12 years.
It contains **so many**
preservatives it still hasn't
started to **decompose**.

A restaurant in Dresden, Germany, suddenly became very **popular** when it started serving up **maggots** on the menu. Dishes included maggot **ice cream**, fried maggots, maggot salads and maggot **cocktails**. It wasn't that the diners **enjoyed** eating the maggots; they just wanted to say that they had **tried** it!

REALLY GRIM BODY FACTS

You have roughly **two** million **bacteria** living on your **face**.

Many people suffer from insect bites while on a **tropical** holiday, but for an unlucky few these bites lead to troublesome **infestations**. One man needed surgery to remove several **maggots** from the flesh of his leg.

Seventy per cent of people confess that they **pick** their noses; worse still, 3 per cent admit to **eating** their **bogies**. Australian Prime Minister Kevin Rudd went one step further on live TV when he plucked some **wax** from his ear to **chew** on while a fellow politician was speaking.

Some people **sweat** copiously and have extra pongy **BO** which has been known to smell as bad as **rotten** fish. This is because they are deficient in a certain enzyme that absorbs the **stinky** protein produced by **bacteria** living in the stomach.

The most prolific **farter** is
thought to be an 11-year-old
who managed to **bottom
burp** 217 times in five
minutes on a **live** radio show.

Your **poo** smells because of two chemicals produced by the **bacteria** in your gut — indole and skatole. Skatole is sometimes used as a **flavouring** in food, and tiny amounts of the artificial form of this flavouring can be found in vanilla ice cream! **Cornet,** anyone?

Have you ever tried to light your **farts**? Some people take this **filthy** habit very seriously, including an elite group of **farters** known as the Royal Order of the Blue Flame.

Your pillow is home to **millions** of tiny dust mites; they provide a great service of **eating** the **dead** skin that you shed **every** night.

Sweet dreams!

A woman in Texas lays claim to the world's *hairiest* tongue. Her tongue has a full covering of follicles, but she **refuses** to have the hair removed as she has been told by admirers that it is **beautiful**.

Mucus from the nose can drip into the mouth and combine with **saliva**. Remember this next time you're **French kissing**!

Sufferers of 'alien hand syndrome' have been known to **completely** lose control over the movements of their 'alien hand', which can feel wholly **disconnected** from the body. There is no known **cure** for the affliction, but patients are advised to keep their hands **occupied**...

The **germs** present in human **faeces** can pass through up to ten layers of toilet paper.

When you speak, you **spray** about 300 **microscopic** saliva droplets per minute — that's about 2.5 **droplets** per word.

The next time you brush your **teeth**, remember to keep your **toothbrush** away from the **toilet**; experts claim that if it is less than 6 feet away, it can become **contaminated** with toilet-related particles.

If your immune system **stopped** working, you would be attacked from within by the **bacteria** that lives naturally in your gut. They would take just two days to **totally** devour you.

If your eyes are feeling **itchy**, your eyelashes could be playing host to tiny **mites** known as *demodicids*. They are **particularly** common in people who do not wash, and heavy **infestations** can lead to your eyelashes falling out.

Mississippi doctors once pulled a **37-foot** tapeworm — the **longest** tapeworm on record — out of a woman's **mouth.**

It is believed that
50 per cent of **people**
who swim in public
swimming baths **wee**
in them too.

A US woman collects **hardened** skin from her friends and family. Some of the prize pieces in her **callus** collection are so large that they are **autographed** by the original owners.

Every time you go to the **toilet**, a small amount of **urine** enters your mouth through your **saliva** glands.

A **tapeworm** was found inside a
woman's brain in Arizona, US. It was
thought to have got there after she
ate **food** handled by someone who
didn't wash their hands after
using the **toilet.**

A 13-year-old boy in India who **unknowingly** ingested some insect eggs along with his dinner later had the **shock** of his life when answering the call of nature. The eggs must have hatched **inside** him as his urine contained lots of tiny winged **beetles**.

Babies are well known for their **dribbles** and messes, and a study found that they produce 38 **gallons** of **spittle** in the first 12 months of life.

During human **pregnancy**, it is possible for one twin to **absorb** the other, the survivor being born with a partially formed **foetus** inside their body.

A US man was able to **exhale** air through his **tear ducts**, enabling him to blow up balloons and blow out candles **through** his eyes.

According to scientists, women's **farts** are smellier than men's, but men produce a greater volume of **gas** – around half a litre per day. Both men and women fart around **14 times daily**, so the number of smelly molecules **emanating** from men and women is roughly even.

You produce enough **snot** to fill a **cup** every day.

Have you ever wondered why your **poo** sometimes floats? Floaters contain unusually high levels of **gas** that the body hasn't been able to **disperse** in fart form, which causes them to **rise** to the surface.

Fancy a cup of **wee?** Some people swear by this for its health benefits and for spiritual **enlightenment.** And sniffing **urine** is supposed to be a good cure for respiratory **problems.**

Every time you sneeze, your body ejects **phlegm**, bogies and anything else that may be **lurking** in your mouth and nose at up to **100 mph**. So put your hand **over** your mouth!

REALLY
GRIM
HiSTORICAL
FACTS

Egyptians in 2000 BC used crocodile dung as a contraceptive.

Ever **wondered** where the expression 'getting your own back' first **originated**? On World War Two submarines, if you **forgot** to close the lid prior to flushing, the **toilet** contents would end up all over you.

In the eighteenth century it was the **height** of fashion for ladies to wear fake **eyebrows** made of **mouse** skin.

King Louis XIII of France had a **toilet** feature built into his **throne** where he would sit while receiving visiting **dignitaries**. Bizarrely, he would insist on eating in **private**.

Sir Walter Scott used
an **unusual** relic
as a salt cellar: the
cervical vertebra
of King Charles I.

In Roman times it was believed that a person could be **poisoned** if they held in their farts. Emperor Claudius was so **concerned** by the potential impact on public health that he passed a law **legalising farting** at banquets.

Perfumes, spices and oils were once a symbol of **status**. King Louis XII of France preferred to **douse** himself in the latest scent rather than **wash** and consequently only had two baths in his whole life — **pooey!**

Death by hand-saw was perhaps the **grossest** medieval method of torture. It involved **hanging** the victim upside down with their legs apart and cutting **downwards** with the saw until the victim was in **two** pieces.

During the Crusades, the problem of **disposing** of large quantities of soldiers' **corpses** was resolved by throwing them into a large cauldron and **boiling** them. The remaining bones were often kept as **trophies** of war.

One of the **goriest** methods for curing gout was practised in the eighteenth century. **Worms** were applied to the affected area and were **only** removed when they had been **dead** for several days and the foul **smell** was too much to bear.

In 1885, the hanging of an Englishman went **horribly** wrong — the jerk of the rope **detached** his head from his body. The executioner had the **unpleasant** job of gathering the bloody victim's body and **head** together again afterwards so the man could be buried in one **coffin**.

Shockingly, during World War Two it is believed that as many as two **thousand** airmen were killed indirectly by **flatulence**. This is because war planes were not pressurised, meaning that at 20,000 feet any **lingering** bottom gas would expand and split their intestines, often leading to **death**.

The ancient Romans used pigeon **poo** as hair **dye**.

Elizabeth I had a peculiar addition to her crown jewels: a gold-framed **bezoar**. These hard bundles of hair and **food** form in human and animal **stomachs**, and at the time were highly valued for their aesthetic and **therapeutic** qualities. Elizabeth's is believed to have come from a **goat**.

Ever **wondered** what people used
before toilet paper was **invented**?
Here are some of the most surprising:

In the Middle Ages, people used **balls** of hay and a **scraper** stick.

In early Hawaii, people used **hard** coconut shells – **ouch!**

French **royalty** in the eighteenth century used hand-made **lace** or **hemp**.

Early Inuits used **snow** and tundra **moss** on their behinds.

In ancient Rome, commoners would use a **sponge** soaked in **salt** water, while the upper classes had the luxury of **wool** soaked in **rose** water.

REALLY GRIM BIZARRE FACTS

On average, women **swallow** about 20 kg of **lipstick** during their lifespan.

What happens when you **wee** in space? NASA has spent millions on resolving the **problem** of what to do when an astronaut needs to answer the call of **nature**. They have devised a method whereby the **urine** is recycled into **drinking** water, called the 'toilet to tap' system.

A pile of **poo** once saved a woman's life in China when she fell from a **sixth** floor balcony and landed on a huge mound of **dung**. She escaped with minor injuries but **smelled** terrible!

It is safer to **kiss** your
dog than your partner; the
majority of humans are
immune to doggie **germs**
and vice versa (but bear
in mind that dogs like
to **eat** cat poo).

One Englishman chose a particularly **gory** way of ending his life; he used a power drill to **bore** holes into his head. It took eight holes to **finish** himself off.

A man in Munich **collapsed** one day and somehow ended up with his mobile phone stuck in his **rectum**. The phone was set on redial to the man's wife and when she **answered** the call she could only hear a strange **belching** sound.

A tenant living in a high-rise flat in Manchester, UK, **abandoned** his 10-foot long snake, who promptly found itself a new home in the apartment block's **sewers**. The boa **constrictor** made frequent appearances in people's **toilets** until a wily tenant coaxed the reptile into a **bucket**.

Some perfumes
and aftershaves use
ambergris, extracted
from the gurgling
digestive system of
a whale, to hold
in the **smell**.

Nine people **drowned** in beer when a vat containing a million litres of the beverage **burst** at a brewery in London in 1814. They must have been **dead** drunk!

In rural Germany, people used to place their **faeces** outside the front of their **homes**. It was believed at the time that the size of the **poo** pile corresponded with the **wealth** of the house's inhabitants.

A **cannibal** put an advert on an Internet message board in 2004, looking for someone to **eat** — and amazingly he got a reply. He and his willing victim first ate the man's penis together before the cannibal killed and ate his **victim**, for which he was sent to jail for **manslaughter** soon after.

Incredibly, a **performer** known as 'The Bottle Man' was capable of dislocating nearly all the **bones** in his body to fit inside a **bottle**.

A US farmer was **surprised** when his chicken continued to **peck** for food after he'd **beheaded** it. He kept it alive by feeding it with a pipette; the bird functioned via the remaining **brain** stem. This 'Wonder Chicken' became a travelling **oddity** but eventually choked to death.

A toad once survived being **swallowed** by a dog. The hound was eating pies that his owner had laid out on the lawn when he **swallowed** the toad whole. His owner rushed him to the vet who induced **vomiting** in the dog, allowing the lucky toad to make a **puke-soaked** getaway!

One Indian man has lived with his **dead** mother for 21 years. He keeps the corpse in a **casket** at home, consulting it to help him make decisions. Lenin, the Russian Bolshevik leader who **died** in 1924, is the most famous embalmed **corpse** and is still on public view in a Moscow mausoleum.

Touching food immediately after handling **money** could lead to infection with an intestinal **disease**. Up to 42 per cent of all paper money is **contaminated** with dirty bacteria and illegal drugs, giving a whole new meaning to **'dirty money'**.

The Madagascan tradition of Famadihan involves **exhuming** the bones of loved ones and **dancing** with them.

A Chinese insect exterminator has a unique method for successful **wasp** removal: he not only catches them, but **eats** them too. The insect lover removes **nests** of wasps from clients' homes without **charging** a fee, so long as he can take the critters home to be **fried** for his tea.

One **unusual** US man had his foot **amputated** and, rather than leaving it to medical science, he put it on permanent **display** on his front porch.

REALLY GRIM ANIMAL AND INSECT FACTS

When threatened, dwarf and pygmy **sperm whales** release a cloud of **faeces** that they hide in until the danger has passed.

Which creature in the animal kingdom produces the **smelliest** farts? The termite, of course! Their excessive **anal** emissions are believed to be a significant contributor to **global** warming.

Being sick is **gross** enough, but it is far worse for a frog. To empty its stomach, a frog will first **vomit** it up then, using its front limbs, it will scoop out the remaining contents, after which it will **swallow** its stomach back down again. This gut-wrenching **phenomenon** is called gastroesophageal extroversion.

The **biggest** locust swarm recorded was 1,800 miles long and 110 miles wide. The locusts **ate** their way through the heartland of the Rocky Mountains and **blocked** the sun for **five** whole days.

A **head transplant** was carried out in 1963 from one monkey to another. The monkey only **survived** for a few days; during this time it was reported to have tried to **bite** the scientists who performed the **macabre** operation.

It's not just a cat's
eyes that **glow**
in the dark – their
wee does too!

The South American candiru fish is particularly **dangerous** to humans as it is known for swimming up openings on the body such as the **urethra**. The fish, with its umbrella-like **spines**, is difficult to remove, and there are reports of unfortunate victims requiring penile **amputation**.

When a hairy frog is **threatened**, it reacts by using a special muscle to **break** its own leg. The broken bone forms a **claw** that pokes through its toe pads, which it can use to defend itself from the **attack**.

A plant in **Borneo** called *Nepenthes rajah* has been known to **eat** small mammals and birds that get **trapped** in its urn-shaped leaves, which can hold over two litres of **digestive** fluid.

The only primate able to **identify** others of its species by their **bottoms** is the chimpanzee.

A type of sea squirt that lives in the seas of Asia performs a **bizarre** rite of passage on maturation: it **attaches** itself to a rock and then devours its own **brain** since it has no further use for it.

To attract **flies** and other creepy crawlies, the carrion flower emits an odour of **sewage**, rotten eggs and **decomposing** flesh.

Ever wondered how your pet might react if you **died**? If your cat was trapped in the house with your **corpse**, it would tuck in and start eating you as soon as it felt **hungry**, whereas a dog would only do so as a **last** resort.

The **mating** rituals of some animal couples can be rather **disgusting**. Here are a few examples of what some **critters** do to attract a mate:

Hippos make their desire known by **weeing** and **pooing** simultaneously. They then swish their **tails** around to **propel** their poo pellets through the water.

A male white-fronted parrot, when feeling **frisky**, will **vomit** up his dinner into a female parrot's **mouth** as a sign of his affection.

The red-sided garter snake will gather up to **25,000** of his snake mates and join together to make a **nesting** ball. Many snakes are **crushed**, but that doesn't stop the males – they will still **try** to mate with **dead** females.

This will make your skin crawl. At any **one** moment, there are approximately 10,000,000,000,000,000,000 (that's ten trillion) **insects** crawling around on this planet. If they were all gathered together, they would weigh **300** times more than the entire human population.

The brown **rat** is so prevalent in the UK that a survey claims you are **only** ever 10 feet away from one in urban areas. With the **total** number of British rats now having reached **60 million**, that's one per person.

Some animals have developed fiendishly **disgusting** ways to protect themselves — here are the **worst** offenders:

The *Phrynosoma*, or horned lizard, shoots **blood** out of its **eyes** by bursting blood vessels in its **sinuses**.

A skunk squirts **vile** smelling gas out of two nozzles inside its **bottom**, and is able to aim the spray in all directions to a distance of more than **10** feet. The spray can induce **vomiting** and short-term **blindness**.

The hagfish, native to the Pacific Ocean, releases a **poisonous** slime when predators come close. The hagfish hopes this will **suffocate** its adversary, but it is also possible for the slime to **kill** the hagfish itself. Afterwards, the deep-sea creature **knots** up its body to squeeze out the remaining **toxic** gunk.

We might think it's the most **disgusting** thing to do, but many animals eat **poo** — and not just their own. These include rabbits, rodents, gorillas and insects such as dung beetles. The poo is not only edible but **nutritious** as it contains intestinal bacteria, vitamins and protein.

But don't try this at home!

Also available:

REALLY
BLOKEY
JOKES

Jake Harris

ISBN: 978-1-84953-185-6

£3.99

Paperback

REALLY CRAP JOKES

Sid Finch

ISBN: 978-1-84953-184-9
£3.99
Paperback

REALLY RUDE WORDS

Sid Finch

ISBN: 978-1-84953-186-3
£3.99
Paperback

www.summersdale.com